# DYING TO KNOW MYSELF IN TIME

# Dying to Know Myself in Time

*Seeking a story
certain of its end
A writer's tale*

HOLLY BRIANS RAGUSA

Amused Moon

Amused Moon
Copyright © 2022 by Holly Brians
Ragusa

First Printing, 2022

Dying to Know Myself in Time
originally was a speech by Holly
Brians Ragusa,
written for a private speaking
engagement given in March 2022 to
students at the University of Con-
necticut Stamford

For everyone, who first, points a finger inward.

Life is not lost by dying; life is lost minute by minute, day by dragging day, in all the thousand small uncaring ways.
-Stephen Vincent Benét

# Contents

Strength

# Strength

What do you see?
What comes to mind?
How does it make you feel?
Don't overthink it.
First thing(s) that come to mind,
Here, in your phone or on paper-
Jot down what you associate with strength.

# Chapter 1

# Who Am I?

I am alive and well today because people believed in me and that belief, that trust, helped me believe in myself. My name is Holly Brians Ragusa.

As a means of introduction, for **better** *and* worse, I will begin by telling you *Who I Am Not*. Notice that I didn't say better *or* worse. I firmly believe there are always (and at least) two sides to any story. Perspective is influenced depending on what side of the trenches we find ourselves.

Now, again, for better *and* worse, who I am not:

I am not patient, I am not an omnivore, I am no longer a friend to some. I'm not a college graduate, I am no longer able to hug my grandparents and I am not a bystander. I am not an employee, not a person afraid of spiders or snakes, not very concerned with sagging boobs, I'm not angry, not religious, not a published book author (YET), and I am not a victim.

*My wildly creative mother-in-law Dona VanAsdale,*
*taught me to say 'Yet' at the end of anything I hadn't*
*yet accomplished but hoped to.*

Who I am, who we all are, is often wrapped up in the "who" we are to others. In these commonly held descriptors, I am a lover, a wife, mother, daughter, sister, niece, cousin, friend, pet keeper, peer, writer, executive board member, trustee, coordinator and community builder. I'm seen as size 8, adult female, cis, white skinned American and blonde.

Call me complex, but I have never been satisfied with these limiting descriptors. As a writer, the words I choose to tell a story matter, especially in the narrative I tell myself.

Who I more accurately identify as; searcher, a life-long learner, a partner and parent, a family ringleader, a grateful traveler, a distracted yet voracious reader, a patron, a poet and bridge builder, an activist and ally. I am an empath and lover of the moon and mustard. I am college educated. I am both a procrastinator and someone who reliably meets deadlines. I am an insomniac who adores sleep. I am a Gemini, who leans a bit Francophile and I identify as a female who feels Freud was right about envy. I'm a believer in science and the seasons. I am into genealogy. I hail from Vikings, Pagans, Protestants, Brittons, Europeans and Scandinavians. I am a United States citizen because my ancestors, some of the earliest European Americans, stepped off boats and stayed on Native land. My family fought on both sides of the Mason-Dixon line. I am the product of a loving mother. I am a creative and deeply connected spirit, who likes both a city and a forest view. A global citizen, I am concerned with hunger, dignity and humanity. I care a lot now about healthy boobs. I'm a lover of history, especially the untold stories. I am a socially active loner, an often childish, greying to white haired, reluctant organizer and I am a survivor.

TO KNOW THYSELF IS THE BEGINNING OF WISDOM.
-SOCRATES

Now that may seem like a lot in the way of an introduction, however, it has helped me to expand on the descriptions placed upon myself, as a human, as a woman, to become entirely aware of who I am as well as how others see me, because that is also me, or the me I am expected to show up as. I need to understand this in order to decide which roles I seek to fill.

*We are no one thing.*

I have yet to decide on a bumper sticker or tattoo; one would limit me, three, four or ten couldn't come close to defining me. I cannot easily separate out certain pieces of myself. I am the sum of my parts. And part of understanding that means that I must reacquaint myself regularly with who I am becoming. I often ask if I am the protagonist or antagonist in my own story.

So that is Me and You are you. Inevitably you may consider your own descriptors, and I encourage you to make note of any that occur to you.

# Chapter 2

# Place

Autumn of 2021, I was at the beginning of a month-long stay in Paris for a long anticipated gift to myself for my fiftieth Birthday. I had decided to embark on an inspirational writer's journey, planned and scheduled nearly 11 years prior (way before Emily in Paris premiered).

Having saved and made arrangements since I turned forty (and despite a delay with the COVID-19 pandemic), the trip was everything I wanted it to be and more. A true writer's sabbatical! In search of inspiration and unsanctioned thought, I relished an abdication of routine and responsibility, and looked forward to encouraging a new reliance on self with the promise of adventure. The trip stimulated my aging (but not old) mind with the challenge of language, location and culture. It was a step outside of comfort and the known. In the end, as much as that trip meant, I soon realized that the decade of anticipation was the greatest gift I had ever given to myself.

For the last ten years, on any given day, if I was down, or stuck, I had that future date and place to look forward to, a dream thumbtacked in my mind to look to in a time of need. Paris was a smile secretly stored away. For some that smile is found on a beach or sailboat. For others it lives in a cabin in the woods. Perhaps it is found on a spice-filled trip to the Middle East, or in a wine glass overflowing in a vineyard. That dream could lie in an ancient ruin or temple...or between pages inside a well-stocked library.

And though, before I'm through, I'd love to smile in all of those places, for me the biggest smile has been and continues to be Paris.

I hope you have or create a place and a date, or the equivalent means of inspiration to envision.

For the opportunity I had in Paris, I am beyond grateful. I do not take for granted the good fortune of affording to go financially with tremendous family support at home. However, without my vision, the saving, the planning, and a commitment to myself to fulfill that dream, I would have allowed a million things to divert me. So I also need to thank *myself* for making it happen, for going, and I need to give *myself* credit, something which can often be difficult for me and I think for many of us.

My first night in Paris, I received what I would call "bad news" along career lines. Tired from travel, a filling dinner and a long late evening walk, I had stayed up to watch The Eiffel Tower fizzle out. Having just gotten settled into bed, I made the mistake of reaching for my phone; that last little check we often make before closing our eyes. There, in that moment, I saw an email slip in from my literary agent. It was two in the morning in France and suddenly I was reading a lengthy email and feeling sick in my gut. My agent was notifying me they felt they had to drop representation of my memoir.

This was the same memoir we'd been polishing, proposing and submitting to publishers for nearly a year. I had worked for four years on writing and editing this story, and my agent, who I truly had faith in, had played a significant role in helping me structure the story better. They helped me understand the maelstrom that is the publishing industry and the humbling and rewarding experience of editing. In this new and swirling pit of doubt, I couldn't even hold anger at this person.

They explained, it wasn't my writing or the story itself at issue, I had feedback from publishers that affirmed that. Lamenting the cause, they explained that the reality of capitalism and the almighty bottom line was to blame.

**The three concerns were:**

First; Sales. Because my memoir wasn't typical or sensational that it wouldn't sell. Couldn't squeeze it into a mold. Had no famous name to slap on its cover or sexy salable tag line to pull readers in. Also, I had no previous sales record to buoy my chances.

Second: Credibility. They said that my subject matter was super unique, but not something I have personal experience in. They suggested perhaps I needed a co-author to bolster sales.

Third: Fame/Notoriety. My agent felt I hadn't grown enough of a platform, or social media following, for my story to be of interest to publishers. A minimum of 10,000 followers was sought, they wrote, while my paltry following sat between 500 and 1700 "friends" on each of several platforms.

****

I'd just been informed that I didn't have the draw or "formal legitimacy of academic or industry expertise". Been told I needed a co-author on *my* memoir; MY life's story. As if I didn't know myself or my lived experience.

So, I sat in the dim with my unpopularity and the gaping hole in my heart at having lost the representation that my business cards and website boasted.

It hurt. Within minutes my ego was a squashed version of its former self. As you may imagine, little rest was had for sleepy, discontented eyes following that news. And as we writers do, I scooched up in bed, sat in the dark, uncomfortably hunched over my phone and laptop, crafting several long (and then longer) versions of response. Drafts of letters, that, after decades of "adulting" experience, I knew better than to send until I'd given them space and time. Thankfully, even in my state of mind, I understood the words needed to take shape in the fog of my mixed emotions.

It is my way. I cannot process life's happenings unless I write life's quandaries down. That night my words were flowing in salty streams of injustice hinting at my emerging potential laced with the appropriate self-effacing and surfacing doubt; we writers are synonymous with imposter syndrome. Still I invoked Salinger and Atwood while climbing hills on principle and digging deep into valleys of craft.

## HOW COULD I *NOT* BE AN EXPERT IN MY STORY?

Didn't my extensive research and archival references matter in something pertaining to me and my family? Didn't I owe more to myself and the story than to sell my soul to sell the story? Who wrote these rules anyway? How disenfranchised should I feel without an agent on this? I mean... Without an agent did I even have (warning: trending word) **agency**?

Despite my mood, in drafts only I was reading, I was still careful not to write anything too damaging. Words matter.

Time (five decades of time) has shown me that restraint assists in how I choose to spin a situation, especially if I want to spin it to my advantage or view it from another vantage. In this case, I didn't want to permanently compromise the agent relationship that had lent much insight and which I had long fought to achieve. If you don't already know, it can take years to acquire an agent in the literary community and it had.

Still, I continued, my words decrying the in-vogue and unfounded formulas for success that many big publishers now look to; driven by followers and dollars. My words mourned the loss of unique literature that so many eyes focused only on shiny objects would surely overlook. Unpopular artists still have a story to tell. Defending my dignity and my non-traditional path, I talked of shedding the costly cloak of doing business as a creative, I broached the issue of how a writer is supposed to write when tasked with first becoming famous.

I mean, my authenticity was at stake damnit!

And while I feel I have a story, and want to share what I consider are my talents, I don't want to waste my time selling myself to followers. Did you know you can

apparently buy followers? I just found out by researching this talk!

Only when exhaustion could not be denied and a
lucid moment alerted me that I didn't have to respond
right away and probably shouldn't, did I find sleep.

And I woke up in Paris.

And that is when I realized;
Paris is *the best* place to receive bad news.

After a shower and a heap of crystalline French butter on yesterday's stale baguette, I stepped at an angle down the winding staircase that had surely stood for hundreds of years despite our efforts. I walked out onto an old street with new stories to tell. A sense of long history mingled with autumnal smells, novel sights and sounds adjusted my perspective in the midday air as I happily drifted away from the news that had kept me awake.

More pressing things mattered than responding to my agent then. I had a city to explore, a month before me on no one else's timeline, where I had only my own wishes and appetites to adhere to. In my entire life, I had never felt this kind of freedom, though my decade long dream surely must have known I wanted to taste it.

I was cut down by this news, and it weighed on me. It felt like a waste, all that time and energy expanded, though, now with the night sunk and a hazy sun overhead, the whole situation appeared less scary and uncertain. The more I walked with this loss, the more it began to morph into an opportunity and options. I began to question things that my "desperate to be published" mind hadn't. Already a sliver of my soul was cheering, glad to be free of the countless revisions and questioning adherence to lower (and lower) word count requirements that had morphed my story into something more palatable for publishers, yet had stolen pieces I considered pertinent in my telling. I longed to add back a few cuts and edit them.

What was this publishing game anyway? And why allow so much rejection and self-degradation at its hands? Self-publishing and Indie-press were options! Walking, I literally laughed out loud at how worked up I had been the night before.

My afternoon slipped easily away on the soles of my shoes as I walked and thought, drifting naturally with the sway of my step in and out of potential and expectation, ego and humility.

I sat outdoors at a bistro watching passerby, while practicing *mon français* and ordering *un café*.

I kept my journal on each table before me, writing as I sat among the intriguing Parisians, listening in and lingering on their accents and mannerisms. I thought of the **powerful gift of time** as I distanced myself further from hurt through that **intentional** act of putting ink to paper. Creating space, pen in hand, I paced within my mind, stopping and settling on **word choice**. Usually I am at my laptop, keys clacking beneath my fingers, and yet, it was pulp and pen that had afforded those we consider *great* across history (Great with a capital G), to stay in our collective consciousness. Writers, politicians, poets, artists, orators, their precious and original words are kept on aging, stained paper, heralded as classic, as our standard (one standard- understanding that so many other words were never able to be written).

Why then had we pushed that level of intention away in literally every area of our lives? History and literature have shown us the restraint of Lincoln and the wisdom of Walden, taking heady steps back to better see what lies ahead, yet today we restrict time allowed for reflection, for major decisions, for love, childhood and parenting. We take less time to appreciate art or dedicate ourselves to a subject.

And, of course it is complicated; we have both enhanced and reduced our ability to better communicate through accessible immediate communication. Harried, fast, without thought, we text in code and innuendo. But...Surely if we have innovations that move at warp speeds, then perhaps we humans don't have to! I sat for a while with my thoughts wondering how I was supposed to be famous before I was well known for anything worthy of knowing.

With that weight on a creative, our work and potential, I fear, can't help but be halved. I found an accomplice to my thinking in Albert Camus, who won a Nobel Prize in Literature, at age forty-four in 1957. He gave a speech, much as I am doing today (without the notable award). His work was titled, *Create Dangerously- the power and responsibility of the artist.* Here I was, living in his country, desperately wanting to do exactly that. Create dangerously. Fall outside expectation, with principal in tact.

*Sad side note: this literary genius tragically died three years later in a car crash.*

After a long walk, and much consideration about what I wanted to share with the world, it occurred to me that it mattered far less *how* I exactly did that than the doing of it. I'd built a map with only one avenue to my goal and had missed all the interesting turn offs that might have gotten me there faster, happier, and calmer.

Returning to my studio apartment, I pulled the best bits from last night's long diatribe, combining a few well-reasoned thoughts into an email to my agent and pressed send.

What I emailed was one of the most honest responses I had ever allowed myself.

And why? Because I had, and gave, myself the benefit of time.

Time, I think, is monstrously over and under defined. If the very wise Virginia Woolf, insists we need a *Room of One's Own*, I'd like to observe that in order for anyone to be effective in that room, it must also have the built in accommodation of free time.

With that long urban walk, I was able to distance myself from initial upset. Creating space, I came to a truly different perspective. By pressing send on the email, I took control, laying those hurdles of hurt and powerlessness behind me. When my agent responded, my thoughts had been honored and validated. Though the result had not shifted, and my work was still unrepresented, my email had been examined and considered, by both of us and my thoughts had indeed been mine. In this awareness, I felt more in tune with my goal.

# Chapter 3

# Time

I gave myself time. Great minds, have weighed in on this weighted concept, this construct. They address it far better than I and in particular, I like Dickinson's and Tolstoy's perspectives here.

TIME ISN'T THE MAIN THING. IT'S THE ONLY THING.

— MILES DAVIS

TIME IS THE WISEST COUNSELOR OF ALL.

— PERICLES

TIME IS A WASTE OF MONEY.

— OSCAR WILDE

TIME MOVES SLOWLY, BUT PASSES QUICKLY.

— ALICE WALKER, *THE COLOR PURPLE*

TO LIVE IS SO STARTLING,
IT LEAVES LITTLE TIME FOR ANYTHING ELSE.
— EMILY DICKINSON

TIME YOU ENJOY IS NOT TIME WASTED.
— JOHN LENNON

THE TWO MOST POWERFUL WARRIORS ARE PATIENCE
AND TIME.
— LEO TOLSTOY, *WAR AND PEACE*

You may be asking yourself, "Why does this matter here?" and "What does it have to do with me?".

I believe time matters more than we often consider.

Our responses are reactions to a world of things that seem to be happening outside of our control. Those responses define us to the world.

Not uniquely, but certainly largely and historically for women, there has been little if any authority over our passions, choices, pay, bodies or time. And though a century has passed with a hard fought right to vote for White women, it has been mere decades with any true representation to legislate and regulate issues specifically facing all women and women have not commandeered full control over any of them. A blip on the screen, a woman's influence on her life.

\*\*\*\*

Just over a decade ago, as I was about to turn 40, I noticed I was becoming unusually angry. It took a while before I understood the cause. See, I was only then beginning to realize the extent of control that had been exacted over me. I was connecting cause and consequence. As I pulled back the curtain, it was definitely a man running the show in a world I had grown into; a world built by and for men.

I started noticing with increasing regularity the misogynist or thoughtless responses from male peers, family friends, even my extended family, noting double standards of care and professionalism. Reading more on feminism, legislation, justice and race, I began to peel back the layers of our historically white, male driven society, releasing that hold over many parts of my life, over my thinking and esteem. Angry for missed opportunities, for thoughts, fears and concerns that had been taught and reinforced in me (holding me back from a fuller life), I felt angry for my children as well. Realizing that not only would time and concerted intention be the only thing to bring about change, I knew that true change wouldn't occur until long after I was dead.

And that quickened the clock for me. It allowed me to see beyond my reality to a future I'd never see. What impact could I have?

Through my parenting I decided it was my duty to raise conscious children. And I think we continue to learn a great deal from each other. Adults often gloss over the wisdom of youth, the clarity of thought that stirs a child's open heart and open hand, untainted by a cynical and limiting society. If we can set ego and certainty aside, there is much to learn about ourselves and each other from young people.

In our family, we educate ourselves and each other about inequity, healthcare differences, pay gaps, biases and micro-aggressions. It is necessary for all genders be equitably treated. We cannot alienate a fraction of the planet. In order to move all women forward, we need our fathers, lovers, brothers, they-dies and gentle-thems, friends, bosses and coworkers to be as invested in balancing out this system as we are. For all of us. Greatness will be found in the skill and talent of our full population, not with some humans placed in power or relegated to the sidelines.

Whatever your gender, time impacts us all in the ever-escalating deadline we all face, of dying. Although time is not unique to females, there are marked differences in how it plays out for them.

Some of the most pressing and life altering decisions have been forced upon women, often made under stress and the pressure of time. It starts young, taking on many shapes, with stakes changing based on the situation. Across our lives it manifests differently; feeling rushed to grow up, forced to show up as something predetermined. With baby dolls placed in baby's hands, already and distinctly women are shown that they are designed to carry and care for others. Then there are the futile years as a preteen wishing to speed up growth to look older, to look more feminine or more experienced.

Perhaps we wish to slow the growing down because we are already attracting attention that we are not ready for. Maybe we are in need of more support and time for our authenticity. Women are disproportionately rushed into sex with higher consequences as data shows the many young single mothers raising our last and current generation.

Even with pressure to marry, birth or advance career or status, research shows child bearers waiting to marry and have children. Now, that we have fought for the space to wait and build our lives, it is our own bodies at odds with us, fighting an ever-expiring timeline to physically bear children, if we choose, and have a good long time to raise them. Our aging itself is often portrayed as a negative, with constant input from marketers insisting we should resist, slow or turn back time with a never-ending multitude of products and surgery options that largely benefit male founded businesses. Time has a deadline, but women have to meet many before that.

Humans are better educated and living longer than ever, yet despite scientific and medical knowledge of the ill effects of stress, we continue to find ways to squeeze ourselves.

Time: It is invariably entwined in our lives and depending how many seconds and minutes we are given, these seemingly **small things add up** and if you are lucky enough to have survived, before you know it, you are middle aged.

Turning fifty made me question: How do I want to spend and use my time? I want to become interesting to readers, and to engage other searchers and thinkers. I want to connect with my fellow humans.

*TIME IS A CREATED THING. TO SAY 'I DON'T HAVE TIME' IS TO SAY 'I DON'T WANT TO'.*

*— LAO TZU*

I can only tell you now at fifty, that it takes a while before I realized the power of time and deliberation on our reactions. I wish you all the streets of Paris for that kind of discovery, but truly, time and space are an entirely new landscape you can each travel your life through. Treating time as a precious resource, as our greatest currency, can provide a very fresh perspective.

In this instantaneous age, we've nearly forgotten *not* to respond right away in a snap, a text or DM. The paradox we buy into is that if we wait too long to respond, we will leave someone feeling unread, worried or wounded. Conversely if we answer right away, we can't think through all of our options and potentially injure or reduce chances to be honest with ourselves and others. We have created our own Catch 22, trapping ourselves.

These fast, quick trigger responses have become innate, a sign of social strength and prowess, of indifference, wit and humor. Thinking our intellect is on display, we ignore the hints of ignorance dropped in the speedy turn of a phrase. What's worse than responding poorly to others, is that we have become careless, thoughtless, even insensitive to ourselves, to our true needs (if, we can even determine what they are).

Despite how deeply a quick response can narrow opportunity, alter levels of professionalism, damage friendships, family and intimate relationships, we routinely do not think about building space before we press send. For the average annoyance or upset, small misunderstandings that occur, are overblown or underestimated, impacting our day, week and month. Overthinking a text without a period or an errant emoji zaps our energy; not in one aspect of our lives, but across many interpersonal relationships!

I think stationary stores need to make a comeback.

Far be it for us, to make others or ourselves wait. How can we possibly ask for a few minutes to think things through before we respond, especially when we haven't operated slowly before? At first, we may confuse people who have become used to our speed, people who have enabled or contributed to our carelessness. To best serve ourselves, understanding what we have allowed to become habit, is of great consequence.

Creating space can be a request for exactly that. "Can I take a minute?" "I need some time before I respond, thanks." "I'll look into that, appreciate the time." "I'll get back as soon as I can.". Better yet, try asking to discuss a complex issue face to face to get a better handle on the situation and to **gauge personal response.**

Time: If we weren't convinced that we had so much of it. If only we understood how best to use it while we do have it. George Bernard Shaw is famously quoted for saying, "Youth is wasted on the young." I'd counter by saying "Time is a bottomless cup for the young." For only age and wisdom understand time's shortage and can wield it effectively.

We are all at the whim of the hourglass. Daily we confront the end of this life, in a seatbelt choice or a sober drive, in fear of sickness, an overpriced insurance policy, in an ignored call from a parent to "be safe", or by living in complete denial.

# Chapter 4

# Death

Death is a very hard topic. Many can't go near it. I find myself far closer to it than others due to personal experience.

In 1986, at age fifteen, I went on a whitewater rafting trip. It was your typical outdoorsy teen summer camp trip coordinated with local churches. After a long bus ride, a fireside campout and a quick safety course the next day, we teens were grouped and put into 5 or 6 small rafts. There weren't enough counselors to have one in each raft, and my raft, the final in the pack, went without. Four fifteen-year-olds were told to paddle. I'll never forget it. We were on the Youghiogheny River in

Pennsylvania, late summer, and the water was below 40 degrees.

Before getting in the water we were told that if we were thrown from the boat, we should stick our feet out in front, and ride the current face up looking at our feet. We had been shown how to paddle in unison on land. And we were cautioned about one particular rapid, Dimple Rock, the most difficult rapid we would encounter that day. Directing us to paddle straight toward the big boulder sticking up out of the water, at a precise moment, when we came up to the big rock, we would then need to paddle hard right in unison, to make the sharp turn. Coming in at the right angle was crucial, or our boat would tip between the boulders.

We'd spent the morning on open rapids, fast but fun. We weren't certain of our skill, but it was exciting. It had recently rained, and the difficulty was a bit higher than the counselors thought, but navigable.

Dimple Rock is a Class 3 or 4 level of difficulty depending on the conditions of the water and as we approached, it became clear that day it was a Class 4. Boulders appeared in the distance and the rushing water grew louder, increasing in volume and intensity as the speed of the river pushed us forward. Being the last boat behind five others, we witnessed the enormous effort needed to make the turn by the other rafts; other rafts with guides.

I was seated in the back on the left. When our boat closed in, and it was finally our turn to navigate this rapid, we all yelled "Here we go!" Someone screamed "Paddle right!" and we did, hard, and to the best of our novice ability. Nervous and ill equipped, we simply couldn't do what the other rafts had. Instead we met the rock head on. The front of the raft slid straight up the rock as it hit, spinning over and downward spilling all of us out. Somehow, everyone was able to pass out in front of the boat. Everyone, except for me. I was trapped, under the boat, and without the presence of mind to have taken a deep breath. The boat had wedged itself perfectly between the rocks. Angled in such a way that I was held beneath it, pressed against the rubber and rock. Forceful water slammed me, and despite my kicking and pushing, I was unable to come up for air or swim under for release.

I can tell you that my short life and a deep sadness for my mother passed through my mind. Literally. Familiar faces floated before me. It was a searing cold, and though I was holding my breath as long as I could I was soon breathing in water, and thinking my life was over.

Just then, the boat lodged free. I burst forth gasping for air, choking up the water that I'd sucked into my lungs. No one times these things, but I was told that I was under for well over a minute, maybe closer to two. It was enough time for counselors downriver to pull their raft over, get up on shore and run up to get as close as they could to Dimple Rock and wait for me to dislodge.

As the racing river carried me forth all I saw after was a white life preserver thrown from shore on a long yellow rope and I grabbed for it, and held on for dear life. I was then pulled over to shore, grabbed out of the water coughing. Land. What a gift. On the damp dirt I was fussed over by the adults. I was alive. I'd gotten lucky. I had not resigned myself to dying, but my mind couldn't believe that I hadn't. My sister, in another boat down river, says she was completely petrified.

According to the Pittsburgh Post-Gazette, since 1976 Dimple Rock has been the scene of count-less accidents in which adventurers in rafts, canoes and kayaks have been caught in the roiling river and flipped into the water. Of the 21 deaths recorded on the lower Youghiogheny River. In the past 30 years, 18 were related to boating, and half of those occurred in Dimple Rock Rapid and nearby Swimmers Rapid. [...] The whirling water slamming into the rock falls back upon itself, creating a "pillow" that can flip boat-ers, pushing them several feet below the surface. The powerful current then can keep them there.

A real brush with death. Whether it is our own death or another's in mind, fear sets in and typically, anxiety and denial follow. Some Psychology class surely has made you all aware of adolescent invincibility or Terror

Management Theory or Social death versus Psychological death. Many of psychology's tenets revolve around dying, they detail our diverse responses to that inevitable fact, that natural cycle of our living with a focus on how we each process old or new loss, or the *time* we could have had with loved ones.

Sometimes a move, or maybe a loss of a job or intimate relationship, can shift our thinking and habits, but often it takes a true brush with danger, severe illness or a meaningful death in our own lives to slow our pace, to bring about an awareness of the precious resource of time. In those instances, the world can feel as if it has stopped. The world stopped for me in that cold Pennsylvania water, and has stopped other times throughout my life when I was in danger or in the midst of experiencing fear or death. Aside from a dead watch battery, death is the only known force that can stop time. Powerful to think of it that way.

****

Dr. Lawrence Samuel, a Smithsonian fellow, writes in a Psychology Today that "If the science of death remains a riddle (we're still not exactly sure why the human body decides to die), the psychology of it has been one of our greatest conundrums. Others die, not us—or at least, that's what most of us like to think." Dr. Samuel goes on to say "We have, in short, a neurosis when it comes to death, with most of us displaying the classic signs of such a disorder (e.g., anxiety, depression, hypochondria) whenever we have to confront the subject in real life."

Fear of death actually shapes many of life's decisions from our connection to faith, to how we vote, even prompting our workout habits and quality of life choices. Death can even be a career choice.

The study of Death: Thanatology. Cole Imperi, a thanatologist, and a very cool cat I met in Cincinnati, focuses not simply on death and dying, but Cole also zeroes in on all loss and how the process of death and loss impacts our lives. Cole is an author and speaker and addresses the little deaths we experience on a regular basis, including physical, ethical, spiritual, medical, sociological, and psychological death. It is a fascinating discipline.

Now, Mortality Salience, or, the awareness of the inevitability of our death, can create a sense of fear and can also confirm our life choices —though there are implications. Studies show that such conformations can actually induce notions of nationalism, or superiority in one's own world view.

However, when we understand that our time here has a deadline, *and* we can envision life beyond ourselves, we can accomplish much good. We can leave meaningful pieces of ourselves.

In researching this talk, I found that Legacy Awareness resonated and, as one article stated, "Why being aware of your mortality can be good for you". The article talked about legacy and how our acceptance of death can actually leave us less afraid and better able to enjoy our time. It can step us outside of the here and now, help us blaze trails, invent solutions or simply display kindness. It discusses how purpose and hope influence our thoughts around death. It discusses the need or wish to leave something behind. Something greater than ourselves.

There are many of us that use our inescapable shared experience, or impending death, to learn, connect, to build bridges, and become more insightful.

Post Traumatic Growth as a concept, comes out of Positive psychology. This thinking is based less in fear than in love or encouragement is and is to my mind, a far more helpful approach. We can see this manifested in Hospice care workers, home caregivers, guidance counselors, service minded staff, therapists and as I mentioned, thanatologists.

Positive psychology is a branch of psychology focused on the character strengths and behaviors that allow individuals to build a life of meaning and purpose—to move beyond surviving to flourishing.

Martin Seligman, often regarded as the father of positive psychology, has described multiple visions of what it means to live happily, including:

- the Pleasant Life (Hollywood's view of happiness),
- the Good Life (personal strengths and engagement)
- the Meaningful Life (insert view of meaning here)

Death has personally impacted me in more ways than a near death experience. My aforementioned memoir was written about my dad. It is a true-crime survival memoir examining my relationship as Dad's step-daughter, and my need to dig into the sensational cause of his death at the hands of a serial killer. Ultimately though, it is my story of facing and overcoming such a traumatic event.

My story doesn't fit into a mold. Life is complex, and this work combines real people and real life stories with true crime, local history, trauma and grief. My work asks the reader to give consideration to the victim and survivors, to shine a light on them rather than a murderer. It recognizes the lifesaving sacrifices of my Mother. It acknowledges my hometown city of Cincinnati and involves our institutions of truth and justice. It deals with the anguish and upheaval of murder, the mental unrest and post traumatic stress that accompanies such an event in a teenage person. And there, I ask us, collectively, to ask more of ourselves.

As an expressive, creative individual, repressing this event was not an option. It was going to manifest itself somehow and often as a younger person, my behaviors were not in my best interests.

# Chapter 5

# My Story

**Tragedy breeds itself.** I state in my memoir.

My trauma response put me on the path for more trauma. Have you ever experienced the difficult journey of pain visited, leading to pain revisited? Informed emotional response is not a day trip destination. Miles of introspection, therapy, patience and forgiveness must be traveled to arrive at a place of peace.

As children we are told to be quiet, to be nice, to play nice. Nice describes being unbothered, it counters "troublesome" people or situations. However, it is not instinctive for everyone to be "nice". Humans get messy in a muddy array of emotions, we cause hurt and act before we access how or others feel. In order to move into "niceness", first, the old boxes of unpleasantness need to be gone through (search, sort, pitch and let go).

Nice is not a character trait; it is a decision.

Schools have yet to teach the most important human lesson; how to express and manage emotions. I have often wondered how the shape of the world might change if we were meeting and treating people based on their experiences, traumas, fears and needs. It is my belief that it could make enormous strides in the quality of life for all to do so. No, I am not carried away by a utopian mindset; there are global benchmarks for it. Commonly held issues could be more justly, humanely and positively be resolved if we looked at each other, our lives, and our minds with a forest management mindset; clearing paths and tackling underbrush. This is a natural form of prevention for inevitable fires that will burn and destroy.

Through the last decade we are beginning to see how Post Traumatic Stress Disorder/PTSD works, not just in our soldiers' returns from hostile climates, but in all people's lives. We have seen in harsh realities of societal violence, how affected we each are by mental wellness, or the collective lack thereof. Treating not only the body, but the mind, is imperative. Understanding what makes us all tick is not just a serious topic of study, but beneficial and applicable in nearly every facet of our lives from understanding ourselves to those we interact with.

The science of Psychology saved me.

Individual and group therapy, intervention, discussion, reflection, and acceptance were the battles I fought in the war with my life. We are often at war with ourselves which causes us to wage battles with others.

I think about that fifteen-year-old me, literally and figuratively trapped under the water. Dad was in the hospital then. He had been in a motorcycle accident and lay comatose. My family and I had been at his hospital bedside all summer. At the time, my sister and I considered not going on this preplanned summer camp, but Mom thought it would be good for my us to have some "normal" teenage time away. On the bus ride down, my sister and I worried together about leaving Mom, but we took comfort that my brother, who was just shy of the age necessary to raft, was home with her. And then, I was trapped underwater, and I remember feeling woefully worried about Mom. Overwhelmed by the thought that my death would cause further heartache during this troubled time with Dad, my thoughts hinged on what me dying would mean to her. This was my clearest and final thought just before I surfaced.

****

That summer before, another brush with danger and water had occurred. Dad, onshore, in his white shorts had been the beacon that kept my eyes focused and my body swimming, when I floated out too far in the ocean on a trip to St. Augustine.

I was fourteen when what began as wave surfing with a cute boy, turned into a mistimed wave ride. Without purchase in the sand I was helplessly pulled away on a strong current.

Despite my efforts, I drifted further and farther from the boy, his face obscuring, then disappearing from view. At one point, I was so far out in the ocean that only the speck of Dad s white shorts held my eyes. But Dad couldn't swim and there was no lifeguard to be found. It was our family's first time visiting the ocean. I never felt more powerless; digging into the water only to be pulled away. I didn't know how to swim parallel to the shore then. I didn't yet know how to go with the flow. The fear that day was so significant, I can almost taste it now. Weary with effort, I was nearly convinced that I might sink or be pulled below, eaten by a shark or die trying to get back to shore.

On the point of exhaustion, a rising wave came toward me. With the luck of my position in the water, the swell pushed me a bit closer toward shore rather than away and I kicked into it. When another wave pushed forward, I swam hard. Another, then another, and on I swam that way, making small but noticeable progress. I could see Dad's shorts clearer. I saw Mom's arms frantically waving as they moved along the beach toward me. Water forced its way into my throat, that unwanted salty chug of sea kept pouring in as I struggled to keep my head and mouth clear of the unpredictable water. That taste of the sea, synonymous with dread for me.

Kicking to stay afloat, all while attempting to keep my eyes ahead and behind, I saw the largest wave yet coming towards me. Timing it, I dug in. Adrenaline kicked in, my arms, turning to jelly. At that moment, threatened, I deliberately forgot my body, becoming sheer will. My heart beat out of my chest. Saltwater challenged the air I needed in desperate measure. Pushing and pulling both in and out of my stinging nose, I kept my mouth pinched shut as much as I could. Forcing myself to make use of momentum with each wave, I pulled myself closer and closer until I could see that cute boy's face clearly standing chest high moving down shore, waving me in.

After a few more cycles of waves, his anxious plea carried across the water to me. On the water's edge, continuing to call and wave, pacing the sand, my family yelled for me to keep swimming. When I finally got close enough, this boy I'd just met, lunged forward grabbing for my arm, yanking me forward. Bobbing underwater to touch the sand underfoot, my tip toes scraped the bottom of a sea that had tested, but not bested me. I remember receiving the incredible gift of structure beneath my feet as I struggled unsteady, to stand.

Atlantic Ocean Florida

Shaky and spent, I trudged slowly the rest of the way to shore, coughing up the sea lodged inside, snot slipping down my face, salt, and gratitude on my tongue. Embarrassed, in front of the boy, my teenage priorities were in full effect. When I got far enough out of the water I collapsed into the shallow waters. My worried family flocked to me, asking why I'd gone out so far... as if I'd planned my watery demise.

Just over a year later my Dad would be severely injured and in his own battle for survival. I would spend my summer and most of my high school sophomore year visiting him in the hospital. Seven months after his accident, Dad would die. Mom would lose her job only ten days later. A week later in our grief we would learn Dad had been poisoned in the hospital bed where he lay.

Two weeks later, an arrest would occur and within two months a story would break our city wide open into an investigation seeking to discover how many other victims fell to the hands of a serial killer. Dad's face and my family would be in the news most nights. My friends wouldn't know how to behave around me. I would be unable to write about what was happening for the first time in my life, dealing with a family undergoing their own grief and turmoil with the wildly fluctuating hormones of a sixteen-year-old.

Underwater just about sums it up.

And yet, I lived. Through those close calls and sadly others. I would live. Whether on open water or trapped beneath it, my watery depths felt out of my control. Life can feel like that. Dad's death felt like that.

But, in living, I had the chance to make new choices.

A year after my oceanic escape, I would avoid that other near-death experience, trapped in a Pennsylvania river's grip. The other teenage girl in my boat had drifted down river and was hanging on a rock in the middle of the river when, our boat, free and rushing downstream, slammed into her leg from behind. She had a nasty gash crushed into her shin bone. The counselors, thankful nothing worse had happened, and desperate to keep their jobs, decided an early lunch would calm everyone and assure the other camp teens about the rest of the rafting day. With only two more rapids left to conquer, a safe arrival at the buses was promised soon. Being very cautious now, the counselors told me that the other girl and I were to wait with one of them. We were informed that we would not be continuing on to the next part of the journey in Tennessee on the New River, but rather a van that would arrive after lunch.

I considered that extraction. Entirely exhausted from the rafting experience, I was also exhilarated and startled to be alive. I remember feeling ravenous!

I knew if I never got back in that boat, no one would think twice. The natural response to fear is to seek safety. Yet, I also sensed that if I did not face and conquer my unease right there and then, that I would forever feel afraid. Fifteen years old, I distinctly knew that I didn't want to live that way; having just been given a chance to do so. During lunch, Dad laying in his bed crossed my mind and I was overcome with his inability to be out in the world, doing what I was doing; experiencing life at this edge.

I decided I'd seen the worst that day could offer.

I got back in the boat.

The counselors and my sister couldn't believe it.

I learned a bit about *Who I Am* on those two water-filled days. I wanted to live, and I didn't want to live in fear. I reaffirmed my strength in being positive, being grateful, and it lent me great perspective.

Whitewater rafting the New River in TN -Holly Brians Ragusa back left of boat-counselor behind

# Chapter 6

# What Brings Me Here?

About five years ago, my oldest child, then twenty years old, faulted me with toxic positivity. Honestly, I didn't know what it was; of course, I googled it immediately. **Toxic positivity** is a way of responding to your own or someone else's suffering in a way that comes across as a lack of empathy. It dismisses emotions instead of affirming them and could come from a place of discomfort, says Tabitha Kirkland University of Washington's Department of Psychology.

Medical News Today defines it thus:

> Toxic positivity is an obsession with positive thinking. It is the belief that people should put a positive spin on all experiences, even those that are profoundly tragic. [It] can silence negative emotions, demean grief,

and make people feel under pressure to pretend to be happy even when they are struggling.

Toxic positivity usually isn't intended to cause harm. Often, it happens in situations when we want to help but don't know what to say, for example, if a friend reveals they received a difficult diagnosis, states McKenna Princing at UW Medicine in September of 2021.

While at times based in cluelessness, habit or lethargy, and intentions can be innocuous, it also is an effective tool used to undermine, control and abuse.

When my child (who has often been way ahead of me on several curves) accused me of this, it was well before the term or the practice of gaslighting were as commonly known or called out. Recently, Merriam Webster made "gaslighting", the word of the year for 2022.

Gaslighting:

1. psychological manipulation of a person usually over an extended period of time that causes the victim to question the validity of their own thoughts, perception of reality, or memories and typically leads to confusion, loss of confidence and self-esteem, uncertainty of one's emotional or mental stability, and a dependency on the perpetrator

2. : the act or practice of grossly misleading someone especially for one's own advantage

- Merriam Webster Dictionary

See, my child suffers from anxiety, and I wanted to be aware of how I was impacting them. Oh, and, absolutely, I saw pieces of myself in that assessment through their eyes.

Classic case.... I had often reassured my child, hoped for better things for them, used positive messages and texts to assure them that things would work out. It hurt deeply to know that my response to their anxiety wasn't helping and may even be hurting. I owned my actions, and acknowledged their response despite knowing my intentions were never meant to harm.

Researching **anxiety**, and reading extensively about it, I assessed my own experiences with it. I began talking with my child and others about it. Then I worked on listening more attentively. I watched my phrasing, focused on pausing, on showing restraint. And I still work at it, continually, because, at my core I am a rescuer. Though I feel a need to be encouraging, if I want to meet my child in a place of love and healing then I have to do so without assuming a positive outcome; even though, through my experiences, that is how I view life.

I've long been comfortable with difficult topics.

Just because I'm on this side of a lot of shit, didn't mean my children were or easily would be. I may have developed some grit, but I couldn't expect my young adult children to. Things are rarely that simple. How could I expect them to understand how to best move forward simply because I had found what worked for me? Who was to say that I had found the best way? I could not fight this or future fights for them. I had to meet them where they were.

That I could hear *need* through this *criticism* was critical to how I responded. My child needed something I wasn't giving. Jumping right over my ego, I ran past my defenses and went right to the core. Empathetically I could then hear this assessment differently. Accusing me of toxic positivity was not intended as an insult, not said out of hate or anger, but said as a statement of urgency, as a request for support- and that moved me to action. Only then was I able to comprehend my full impact. Only then could I grasp that I was the only thing standing in the way of changing my response. Largely I have changed it, and I continue to read, breathe and work towards a stronger relationship with both my children. I hope to be asking more of myself for the rest of my days.

I remain a positive person. I believe the best in people, I do not by nature assume the worst. I hope for better things because without hope I wouldn't be here but I don't assume bad things won't happen or don't affect us. I do not believe in repressing.

Recently I read an article on **Tragic Optimism** by Scott Barry Kaufman in *The Atlantic,* August 2021. The antidote to toxic positivity is "tragic optimism," a phrase coined by the existential-humanistic psychologist and

Holocaust survivor Viktor Frankl. Tragic optimism involves the search for meaning amid the inevitable tragedies of human existence, something far more practical and realistic during these trying times.

Researchers who study "**post-traumatic growth**" have found that people can grow in many ways from difficult times—including having a greater appreciation of one's life and relationships, as well as increased compassion, altruism, purpose, utilization of personal strengths, spiritual development, and creativity. In a book titled *Post-traumatic Growth: Theory, Research, and Applications* (1st edition) by Richard G. Tedeschi, Jane Shakespeare-Finch, Kanako Taku and Lawrence Calhoun, it was important to note that it's not the traumatic event *itself* that leads to growth (ie: no one is thankful for COVID-19), but rather how the event is processed, the **changes in worldview that result from the event**, and the **active search for meaning** that people undertake during and after it.

This Tragic Optimism really resonated with me, having gone through my share of hard things while seeking reason or purpose throughout my life. This perspective more closely defines what I often intended to convey to my oldest child. There is unequivocally going to be adversity in the business of living. Despite my parental wish that my child would not have to experience misfortune, mayhem or heartache, they simply would. We all need to suffer to grow.

We cannot be told how to go through difficulty. Every one of us must figure out these things for ourselves. Oh, it will look wildly different to each of us, however, I have discovered that if we search ourselves for it, meaning can be found in that suffering. Meaning that matters. Given the past couple of years of the pandemic, societal and global issues that we have all witnessed, the searching for meaning within ourselves and from our times, continues.

****

I am 35 years past Dad's death and it is something I'll never be over. And that is ok. It is said that grief is unexpressed love. Grief is the vehicle we drive to arrive at the irrevocable terms of death. Personally, I feel grief often like that ocean, pushing and pulling. Exactly like a wave mounting an overwhelming attack on us, as fear and regret slam into us. Memory can bring us to a depth beyond imagining, then miraculously return us to the surface. In accepting, grief slows the tide, ebbs and steadies, and can even bring us placid peace. My grief, my process, have all become a part of who I am and my memoir simultaneously acknowledges my vulnerabilities and my strengths. After this much time, I have learned they are not so far apart.

How we view strength matters.

Turn to your initial perceptions on strength and re-member what images or associations came to mind.

Power. Endurance. Patience. Resilience.
Perseverance. Steadiness. Power. Money. Might.
Muscle. Brawn. Manliness. Lioness.
Destruction. Devastation. Decisiveness.
Mother Bear. Mother Nature. Elemental Forces.

Perhaps you attached to other qualities
or even assigned specific people as strong.

Maybe you see the subtleties of strength standing up-right through tear filled eyes, facing fears, or bravely having difficult conversations. You might have listed a person who represented fortitude or inspiration such as your mother, father, friend or grandparent. These are all worthy, we each see strength present itself in differing ways. Our upbringings might have confused us. Many see crying or overthinking as weaknesses, removing in-tellect and empathy from our consideration. I think for most of us it is easy to overlook courage in ourselves, difficult to recognize our own strengths.

On my card, I wrote that strength is - "Asking for help"- because for me, it is the one of the hardest things I can do.

I consider opening up and crying on a friend's shoul-der to be a sign of strength. I would also consider being that shoulder for someone else, a strength. I consider facing your true self in the mirror to be an act of great bravery. Forgiving yourself may be the greatest strength of all. Once we forgive ourselves, we can begin to forgive others and value the lessons we've learned. I would say that committing to being your most authentic self in a world that might otherwise marginalize you, is an absolute strength.

# Chapter 7

# Following Legacy

NO LEGACY IS SO RICH AS HONESTY.
-WILLIAM SHAKESPEARE

I'M NOT INTERESTED IN MY LEGACY. I MADE UP A
WORD: 'LIVE-ACY.' I'M MORE INTERESTED IN LIVING.
-JOHN GLENN, AMERICAN ASTRONAUT

PEOPLE WHO THINK YOU COULD
WAVE A MAGIC WAND AND THE LEGACY OF THE PAST
WILL BE OVER, ARE BLIND.
- RUTH BADER GINSBERG, SUPREME COURT JUSTICE

I'M ATTENDING TO MY LEGACY, MAKING SURE
THAT IT TRAVELS THE UNIVERSE IN THE BEST
SHAPE I CAN GET IT INTO. FOR AS LONG AS I'M
ALIVE, I'LL STILL BE ITS INTERPRETER.
-ROY HARPER, MUSICIAN

NO MATTER WHAT HAPPENS IN LIFE, BE GOOD TO
PEOPLE. BEING GOOD TO PEOPLE IS A WONDERFUL
LEGACY TO LEAVE BEHIND.
- TAYLOR SWIFT, MUSICIAN, MOGUL

YOU WRITE IN ORDER TO CHANGE THE WORLD ...
IF YOU ALTER, EVEN BY A MILLIMETER, THE WAY
PEOPLE LOOK AT REALITY, THEN YOU CAN CHANGE IT.
- JAMES BALDWIN- AUTHOR, ACTIVIST, INTELLECT

Legacy is what we leave behind and how we want to
be remembered. How then, do we leave or live a legacy
within the time we have?

## How do we *matter*?

As you may have noticed I have a deep respect for the
words of others. Most writers I know do. When it comes
to legacy thinking, brilliant minds across time have made
their own worthy assessments, and I pause to hear their
wisdom as I consider my own.

We must understand that our name is tightly bound
to our character, our actions. And yet we can't only live
for how we will be seen tomorrow, nor can we deny the
past and its implications. We must tend our garden, and
cultivate our growth. As the bright light of Dr. Maya Angelou said, "people may not remember what you said, or

what you did, but they will never forget how you made them feel".

My story is at odds with my platform and my platform is not supportive or indicative of the strength or power of my story.

Because of who I am and what I have endured, perhaps my perspective is skewed. A wise and dear friend recognized the late bloomer I am, encouraged me to step into myself. Since I find myself here, late, but not too late to the party, I am able to question and discern other paths. I can both invent and circumvent ways toward my goal. Do you want to stand out in ways that are meaningful? I do. I want to help us see pieces of ourselves in each other, to share in the hardship, unique beauty, and resilience of the things we weather.

We stand on a foundation and will someday be buried into collective wisdom for future generations. Every bit of knowledge adds to the whole.

I am not insignificant despite my lack of fame or followers (I know that), though we can often be made to feel that way in this society. My head certainly veered in that direction in Paris, after that email from my agent. But I pulled myself back, I reflected. Ultimately, fame was never my goal. My wish was to move others with my words. With space I was able to see that I can achieve that through my work in every personal or public inter-action. Finding purpose, leaves me feeling significant.

I don't need to follow anyone else's path; though plenty of us have blazed worthy and wondrous trails. Blending in is not an activity I strive for and, neither, have I raised my children to do so. Breaking out from the herd though, does not necessitate leaving the flock. If I have a network, no matter how small, I can lever-age it. We writers are reliant on community, for support, but also for troubleshooting, referrals and reviews. Our support systems are tight or wide, they vary in scale and scope, yet each of us relies heavily upon each our literary herd.

Lately, I hear folks labeling other folks as sheep, with a negative connotation (often relating to politics). I can-not imagine the lack of awareness in casting that stone without accepting it as a truth largely held by the major-ity. Sanctimoniousness or hypocrisy are rarely a helpful tacts. If we look past blame, it is apparent that most of us feel safer within the fold- in whatever fold accepts us. But safety is not assured when social media becomes our shepherd.

I am more socially active than either of my two grown children. My youngest opts in lightly to social media to promote their own creative work. My oldest child, years ago; foreseeing the algorithms, biased target-ing and tracking that would become the fox in sheep's clothing that would likely tear us apart; shuns it entirely on principle. Wise, that one.

But I admit, I am addicted (with a capital D for dopa-mine) to the connection, to knowing what is happening in my friends' lives, in my community and in the world. It makes events easy to track and find, I see breaking news on what I consider reputable outlets there. Poetry readings, author signings and literary community is built online. I keep a finger on the pulse of my world. Under-standing the risks, I work to mitigate them by educating myself outside of these portals, and while I am not per-sonally averse to social media, I am also not naive to its drawbacks.

> When my agent said I didn't have enough followers...
> Only then did I realize I didn't want to be one.

Elizabeth Harris wrote in *The New York Times,* an article in December of 2021, that jolted me so shortly after my agent's reasoning.

*"Millions of Followers? For Book Sales, It's Unreli-able.* Asking "Social-media fandom can help authors score book deals and bigger advances, but does it translate to how a new title will sell?" Publishers are increasingly skeptical."

Numbers do not support the thinking that is driving my former agency (I could not help myself and sent this article to my agent a few weeks after that Paris email). On Instagram, I currently have an onslaught of bitcoin sellers, divorced international singles and business owners asking to follow me. Do you think that if I added them into my followers, to inflate my numbers, that they would purchase my book were I to promote it there? I don't think so.

We all have to figure out what being famous now means. Are we a promotor? Do we have sway? When fashion, fad, fantasy, farce (or a daily dance trend) can garner 2 million followers on TikTok, when you can make a decent living as a sponsored YouTube (er), we cannot shun the importance of a "Like and subscribe" request.

Those of us on social media choose to follow famous figures, periodicals and topics of interest. Easy target, I am a pushover for dog and cat rescue videos, marine life, travel and landscape photography. Humor helps me feel less alone with perspectives from nighttime show hosts and comedians, and I really like the 'living off the grid' folks and DIY tiny homes and renovations. Yes, I follow and cannot escape entertainment news and sensationalism. Still, I will always lend more weight to a Nobel Prize winning scientist, literary genius or environmentalist than a mere personality. Experts deserve the largest followings. Disseminating information relevant and fascinating to our living, scientists, artists, medical professionals and engineers can draw us together through knowledge. With access to qualified research and skill, society gleans information, makes adaptations, and creates solutions.

History... or **stories of time...** will show us that names will never surpass stories connecting us to each other. Without a story, a name is simply that.

Yet we live in a digital age and we are all at the whim of learning how to best wield this new data and influence. We must evaluate our own worth and fluff or flounder our esteem as we gain access into the lives of people and their preferences and ask: How we are helping? Often, these beautiful, rich or famous faces are filtered to reflect our lamest selves back to ourselves. Be aware of what helps and what hurts.

Older generations see the game very differently and are not as savvy to algorithms that are targeting them. Anyone uniformed or unaware of their own marketability may be easily manipulated, and especially for our aging population; what was printed was deemed true when they grew up.

Faith, for many, is at the heart of this nation and religion has always relied on messaging. Each brand of faith steeping generations in love and fear, pitting pulpit against pulpit.

WORDS ARE FREE. IT'S HOW YOU USE THEM
THAT MAY COST YOU.
-REV. J. MARTIN - JESUIT PRIEST AND AUTHOR OF
*BUILDING A BRIDGE: HOW THE CATHOLIC CHURCH AND THE*
*LGBT COMMUNITY CAN ENTER INTO A RELATIONSHIP OF*
*RESPECT, COMPASSION, AND SENSITIVITY.*

Often and not only in my line of work, I am reminded of how deeply words matter. Long-time family friends have split over hurtful comments. Families are broken by lies and political information and misinformation. Love is deepened in a penned letter or in a spoken proposal. Across time, the power of gods has been believed and fortified from myth, fable and sermon. Nations are inspired by impressive oratory, and countries declare rights for their citizens with word and deed.

Words: Humans can be desperately wounded by rounded letters pulled together into sharp sentences. Uplifting or injurious phrases from those we love and admire or spewed discontent from the "haters", both sentiments stick with us, repeat in us, and re-injure. Constantly we prove ourselves "right or wrong" by what is said or written.

Dividing ourselves into what we admonish and what we praise (and never the two shall meet unless over a TikTok dance or animal video), our content- we have decided, should astonish, startle and entertain us, but not make us too uncomfortable. But, push the boundary of our beliefs, and facts be damned. I think we are the poorer for it.

# Chapter 8

# How We Talk To Ourselves Matters

THERE IS AN OLD TSALAGI OR CHEROKEE TALE

"A Cherokee elder was teaching his young grandson about life.

"A fight is going on inside me," he said to the boy. "It is a terrible fight and it is between two wolves. One is evil- he is anger, envy sorrow, regret, greed, arrogance, self-pity, guilt, resentment, inferiority, lies, false pride, superiority, self-doubt and ego.

The other is good- he is joy, peace, love, hope, serenity, humility, kindness, benevolence, empathy, generosity, truth, compassion and faith.

This same fight is going on inside you—and inside every other person, too."

The boy thought about it for a minute and then asked his grandfather, "Which wolf will win?"

The elder simply replied, "The one you feed."

- *A Tsalagi Tale*


Understanding how we speak to ourselves can truly help us stay afloat. Considering, that the responsibility we owe to ourselves is often wrapped into clichés or simplified into self care conversations and memes, we might need to explore what talking to ourselves means.

I have found that it is easy to beat ourselves up, delicious to beat others up, and a challenge to call ourselves out in ways that will bring positive change. Responsibility goes over well when casting a stone in another's direction or in blaming ourselves without a plan to move forward. Calling ourselves and each other "stupid" won't change that assessment. Reconciling and evaluating our own behaviors and accountability, will. Shame settles in us for wrongdoing, for missteps, for other's perceptions. Until we review roles, accept consequences, and forgive or ask to be forgiven, shame spreads its dark ground covered mass over our ability to grow.

Digging into our darkest parts is never easy. And, there is always a "better time" to do that work. However, the longer that work is put off, the more it festers, the more it eats away at us, the longer we build unhealthy habits.

LIFE BEGINS AT THE END OF YOUR COMFORT ZONE.
-NEALE DONALD WALSCH, *CONVERSATIONS WITH GOD*

**Life begins at the end**.... I love just *that* part of this quote.

With appreciation for the paths we all walk, I am in awe and astonishment of the dangerous and daring magnitude of steps that lead us to our differing and often entrenched positions. In acknowledging that we start with the path we are born into, not of our choosing, shaped by early environments and belief systems held there, it only follows that we are moved along a pendulum of thought and feeling by the experiences and exposures we have.

Many of us think we are "good people" and have designated others as "bad".

I tend not to see things in that binary way. The incongruent definitions we apply to these words of good and bad, cannot allow these words to stand as pillars. I have resolved that we cannot know one without the other, the light cannot exist without the dark.

Balance is necessary. Not only do I *not* mind different opinions, I thoroughly enjoy hearing them, discussing and debating, researching and expanding on those opinions. **Nuance is no enemy of mine.** However, I do mind greatly when opinion oppresses or injures others. Though - I will note that many of us have a limited understanding of how greatly we impact, injure or affect those around us.

As a woman, I often reflect on that full impact, our effect on others, and not just in our expected or projected appearances but also in the workplace, in our friendships, with intimate partners, through parenting and nurturing, and how we find place in community. Understanding our impact upon each other is revealing. Yes, notoriously, we women do not defend each other, and also yes, in this still standing patriarchy, we are complicit.

BE CAREFUL HOW YOU TALK TO YOURSELF,
BECAUSE YOU ARE LISTENING.
-LISA HAYES

I am interested in knowing our impact on ourselves, on our hearts and minds, on what we tell ourselves. How we frame our thoughts, our experiences, our suffering. I am listening to every word, and whether or not you know it, you are too.

Think of all of the harmful things

we tell ourselves.

*I am not smart enough, not rich enough,
not connected enough. I am too fat, too thin,
too stupid. I can't get anything done. I will
never make that deadline. I'm not
interesting. No one wants to hang with me.
No one will ever love me like that.*

In these descriptors we are literally defining ourselves. We are telling ourselves who we are. We are saying we are unintelligent, untrustworthy, undesirable. Things we would never say to a friend. Do we need to heap more onto our piles? What if we were our own best friend and treated ourselves really special?

I often date myself. Truly. Not just in Paris, but since I was in high school. I would take myself to the movies or dinner. Alone. I'd bring a book to a bar if I wanted to relax with a drink. Loving yourself extends into each minute we are alive. If we want love, we must first love ourselves, unconditionally, entirely, not blindly.

> Treat yourself the way you want to be treated by others.

In any intimate friendship or relationship where our heart is tethered, we must understand who we love, to know how we can best love them. This is no different in our relationship with ourselves. I have learned to truly enjoy my own company, not to despair when a friend runs late, not to feel lost without others, but to take time to breathe into who I am today.

I've gotten to the point where now, if I'm taking a walk and I just want to stop and soak up a lovely moment, I will text that I may run a few minutes late. This extra minute allows me to experience the beauty in an otherwise rushed day. It is unusual for me to make my friends wait more than a few minutes, but now and again, it important to place yourself in the position to receive a gift from yourself. I don't encourage being late for work or class; surely stress will then enter in, but overall, easing up permits ourselves more time. Before and after work, seek these moments, allow time to enjoy *being*. It is easy to get down on ourselves and call each other out, however, we can also remind ourselves to extend and share love.

So, without promises, fluffing or over-inflating, what types of real-life things can you say to yourself that may be helpful or goal or solution oriented?

Examples:
Take a deep breath, you gave it your best.

I can try again tomorrow.
I can be more tender.
I'll read one book a month.
I do take care of others.
I'll start taking long walks on Sundays.
I'll give myself 15 extra minutes of sleep each night.
I'll prepare two healthy meals a week.
I'll cut back costs on take-out.
I'll try reading a different news source each week.
I will wake and think of three things I'm grateful for.
I am at my capacity for now.
When able, I will give more.
I'll forgive myself when I do none of these things.
I can start again.
I am trying.

Any effort, no matter how small can make lasting change. Think of an instance where someone made you smile, or a time when you made another person smile. That same smile moves through a day, worn on many faces, originating with one person who decided that it might make them feel better to make someone else feel better. Intention. Energy. Flow. Get into your own flow, discover language that resonates in you effectively, authentically.

# Chapter 9

# Experience +
# Belief = Life

We cannot overlook the importance of faith, spirituality or religion in our conversations with self, around purpose, about time or our finitude. Fundamentally, faith understands that suffering is a part of life. Each dogma, creed or doctrine, ascribes tools to function within a mortal reality, with the divine in mind. Inevitability seen through the lens of belief.

Heaven and hell transport and tame us.

Whether your spirituality lies in a prescribed faith, is widely understood, shared in wide fellowship, or resides intimately within your own heart and mind; belief guides purpose. Belief leads us simultaneously on strikingly different and commonly used paths. Pain pours through our chosen or learned belief systems, resulting in varying responses when layered upon our subjective experience. When we accept our inevitability, we can better extend reason, empathy, perspective and solutions to our problems.

Religion is not the same as spirituality. How you grew into faith and even how you may have drifted away are part of your spiritual path. If your soul seeks a deeper spiritual connection, a world of options are yours to explore. Sacred texts, traditions, ceremonies and holidays can pull us into a chosen path of enlightenment, fellowship or propel us into peace and solitude. I have found that what we believe is at times less important than believing. Belief upholds us, inspires us and connects us. Create a space that brings you calm, that holds you in the beauty of your truth.

****

Where we see ourselves in life also matters. Perhaps age, capability or career path means that the focus needs to be on you right now. Or maybe family and friends receive the benefit of your full attention. Perhaps, for the moment and for your own well-being, the focus cannot be anywhere except on yourself. Our energies each spend and operate differently. Assess where you have been and where you are. Understand that tomorrow may find  you elsewhere.

Seeing a way forward for ourselves, let alone our loved ones, may seem daunting or even unattainable. Paving the way for others brings purpose to some, yet does not serve others. No matter our focus, no matter the issue, in any instance, whether we act or not, leaves a mark.

Quite simply, I choose to act in my belief that we are all connected in this full-scale production called life.

\*\*\*\*

In our collective and upheld canon, there is a well-known and oft repeated summary of life through William Shakespeare.

> All the world's a stage,
> And all the men and women merely players;
> They have their exits and their entrances;
> And one man in his time plays many parts,
> His acts being seven ages.

> At first the infant,
> Mewling and puking in the nurse's arms;
> And then the whining school-boy, with his satchel
> And shining morning face, creeping like snail
> Unwillingly to school. And then the lover,
> Sighing like furnace, with a woeful ballad
> Made to his mistress' eyebrow. Then a soldier,

Full of strange oaths, and bearded like the pard,
Jealous in honour, sudden and quick in quarrel,
Seeking the bubble reputation
Even in the cannon's mouth. And then the justice,
In fair round belly with good capon lin'd,
With eyes severe and beard of formal cut,
Full of wise saws and modern instances;
And so he plays his part. The sixth age shifts
Into the lean and slipper'd pantaloon,
With spectacles on nose and pouch on side;
His youthful hose well sav'd, a world too wide
For his shrunk shank; and his big manly voice,
Turning again toward childish treble, pipes
And whistles in his sound.

Last scene of all,
That ends this strange eventful history,
Is second childishness and mere oblivion;
Sans teeth, sans eyes, sans taste, sans everything.

And whether one believes in oblivion or an afterlife, what is the point of comprehending these ages of life unless we have purpose, love, passion and a deadline to meet them all? First, none of us are guaranteed any of these stages. Personally, for where I am in life; for the years acquired and health maintained, for the dangers and pitfalls I narrowly avoided, for the people I have in my life and for who I have become; my gratitude is immense.

Gratitude has become the brightest star in my galaxy; serving as a beacon, a practice, a therapy. My Mother's gift for appreciation is innate and wakes her each day, yet it took me years to develop my own thankful mindset. I intentionally built that perspective into my living and I choose to look through its less cluttered lens.

Once, I read that to wake and consider three grateful thoughts before beginning the day would steer a course away from feelings of despair. So, I tried it, again and again, reminding myself to think of three things for which I felt privileged to have in my life. Different people and things presented themselves each day while I formed the practice as I woke. Eventually, I didn't have to remind myself to think of three things. It isn't always easy, and I don't automatically go to gratitude, but when I'm really down, and hope dims, I always seek gratitude's light and it awakens a helpful and purpose filled mindset within me.

I know this, about and for myself, **time and attention matter.** I have learned how rare and precious life is. There can never be enough of it and yet rather than live in denial, I live in full awareness of its limits. Any attention I lavish on people or purpose demonstrates my greatest investment with the most meaningful currency, **the currency of time.** How we spend it on ourselves and others is consequential. Tendering control over any other aspect of time is futile.

The future cannot be realized by worrying over it or wishing for it. We are here, for unknown measure. Life, being the greatest of all adventures, **will have a start and an end**. With a deadline in mind, I am motivated to use time how it serves me best, building space into a full calendar for myself and others, breathing into a day, easing into an evening and making allowances specifically for creative time and spontaneity.

Interacting, learning, leading, knowing, and participating, these things I subscribe to - not following. I certainly don't want others to merely follow me either. Interaction is how I wish for others to participate in my life and I hope that people who choose to "follow along" with me on my journey, would have my best interests at heart. I hope a cord of connection will be tied to what I am putting out into the world. This is why I follow along with others, why I invest my time in their life stories, and why I feel compelled to share mine.

THE WORLD IS FULL OF STORIES,
AND FROM TIME TO TIME,
THEY PERMIT THEMSELVES TO BE TOLD.
-OLD CHEROKEE SAYING

When my agent told me that I had no professional or credible experience in the area of my memoir, it got me thinking seriously about that.

# Chapter 10

# Who I Want to Be
# -versus- Who I Am

It had taken me 30 years to begin writing about everything that had occurred with Dad's death, how I'd processed such a thing and become collateral damage to actions outside of my control. My memoir is entirely about taking back the narrative. Assembling my thoughts and experiences helped me see, from a birds' eye view, life, for the web of connection life is.

We all have trauma.

When I was sixteen, I promised myself and Dad's murderer, in an unsent letter, that I would discover everything I could about those murders in order to make some sense of it all. Three decades passed and I had only made half efforts and delayed the work. Within me though, a need to fulfill that promise never faded. At age sixteen, at my core, I already knew who I was, though I spent my twenties and thirties doubting it.

In my early twenties, I met and married a magnificent partner. My husband and I work really hard at our marriage and have raised two really neat kids into unique, creative adults. Having committed to setting the example, I always tell my children, "Find your equal!", and they seem to have done exactly that. I cannot gloss over the tremendous amounts of joy and struggle that come with a committed relationship. I appreciate the work opportunity and happen to be in love with my co-worker.

As our children grew older, I found more time to myself. When my teens turned to their rooms and their friends, that original promise to myself at age sixteen, to write about my life, crept back into my mind. I spent the last five years writing a story that brings me to today. My writing effort, paired with extensive research, two major structural editorials, insight into my craft, two dozen revisions, at least 10 mental wellness breaks, countless line edits - was accomplished and I had finally done it, I'd finished the manuscript.

The sense of reward at this triumph was, and is remarkable. Healing through the process of writing remains the undeniable gift. I feel a powerful need to share my story. And while my memoir is complete, it will never be fully finished, as art is never finished. Each of our stories are constantly evolving. Writing my memoir, seeking publication, and continuing a path toward growth, has become a side story (or perhaps the main storyline).

*update: after enlisting a fabulous editor, and going through three more revisions, Met the End was self-published November 2022!*

When you realize how you want to be remembered, the narrative shifts. We all leave pieces of ourselves in this life, on this planet, that live on in memory and deed. Though some of us are household names, well known and famous, we can't all accomplish that. Still, I think it is important to add to the collective pile. I believe that each of us matters, that each person we interact with matters.

Realizing the importance of knowing myself within the time I have, I am sharing my lived experience. Knowing *Who I Am* and how much it intersects with *Who I Want To Be* means that each day I am getting closer to a goal.

I cannot get a degree in life... yet!!

There are likely few certificates that can determine my level of expertise. My three and a half years at college didn't produce paper. My **trauma didn't provide** me with a plaque on a wall. However, there are many among us without pedigree or certification, autodidacts who perfected their craft and have made considerable contributions.

Famous, well-known names add in, with magnificent and profound reach: William Blake, George Washington, Harriet Tubman, Abraham Lincoln, Frances Ellen Watkins Harper, Mamie Smith, Oprah Winfrey, Bill Gates, Malcolm X, George Orwell, Stephen Foster, Kobe Bryant, Jimi Hendrix, Frank Lloyd Wright, Nicola Tesla, Karl Marx, Benjamin Franklin, Ray Bradbury, Richard Wright, Maya Angelou. These famous individuals are known through their wonderful inventions, beautiful poetry, fantastic designs, stellar films, profound philosophy, lasting justice work, and deeply imbedded music and artwork. These people are not known for their college degrees. In fact, some were bestowed that honorary title for their contributions outside of academia that cannot be ignored. Cultures have **benefited enormously from non-traditional paths** and we must recognize the simple fact; there is not one path that will suit all. Let us widen the avenues for learning and innovation.

Most repeated advice I offer to my children:
Seek Balance.
Find Your Equal.

I worked hard to find both. Balance, I think, is a tightrope act we all continually walk. We cannot seek to fulfill other people's visions of our possibilities (or the *tyranny of potential* as my astute other mother-in-law, Elizabeth Yarris, Ph.D., a counseling psychologist, described it). I knew the balance I sought in my life, my mind. And without any formal degree, I know that I am a survivor.

# Chapter 11

# Survival

TO LIVE IS TO SUFFER,
TO SURVIVE IS TO FIND SOME MEANING IN THE
SUFFERING.
–FRIEDRICH NIETZSCHE

ALTHOUGH THE WORLD IS
FULL OF SUFFERING, IT IS ALSO FULL
OF THE OVERCOMING OF IT.
–HELEN KELLER

OUT OF SUFFERING HAVE EMERGED THE
STRONGEST SOULS; THE MOST MASSIVE
CHARACTERS ARE SEARED WITH SCARS.
–KHALIL GIBRAN

Famous quotes are not going to solve your problems. Words can hurt and won't make everything magically

better - however- words will put a brain to work considering options. Though blind to options when trapped
or feeling stuck, they are there waiting to be discovered,
offering chances. Taking those chances is how survival
happens.

Putting thoughts together, no matter how inconse-
quential they appear, is the first step to getting out of
one situation and into a better one. Intelligence understands that no one has all the answers (let alone any one
of us in isolation). Support is out there waiting, often
not in the shape we expect it. If friends or family are
not accessible, seek outside resources. Search between
countless pages. Find inspiration where you will, there is
only a shortage of vision and exposure.

Choose what to feed your heart and mind.

As a teen, my mother and I were asked to speak on
the death penalty to a group of students at The University of Cincinnati. We were more than a parlor trick, we
had skin in the game, having lost someone to homicide.
To make matters interesting, we were on opposite sides
of that debate. The person who led our support group of
survivors asked if we might contribute to the class with
our unique experiences and with coaxing, we agreed to
participate. We discussed our loss, shared our perspectives and answered questions. The students were attentive, engaged in our life story, and found themselves on

both sides of the issue seeking a foothold on the topic. Connecting the intensity of our views with the students' curiosity and uncertainty about the penalty of death, Mom and I were able to personalize the issue for them. Thankfully, at the time, we were the closest exposure to murder for the students in that class. After all these years, I treasure a stack of handwritten thank you letters from a collegiate class written to my mother and I. At the tender age of eighteen I was an expert in both life and death.

And many of us are. **Our lived experience matters.** Our stories matter and with this wide world waiting, there are thankfully a million ways to share them.

That was the first talk I gave around this very personal event in my life. You may be surprised, but sharing deeply personal information can be very liberating. When there are no secrets, there can be no shame and without shame, we get to look on our choices with a full heart- we get an aerial view of our efforts and can respond with empathy and grace - the same grace we would extend to those around us, we find difficult to supply ourselves.

Common threads bind us to the pained smiles and vacant faces we see everyday. Every heart that feels burdened, every mind that weighs heavy, feels alone.

We are a web connected, feeling similar joys, pains, losses
and isolations across the entire globe. We are stronger in

some places than others, we are weaker for a while after a storm rolls over us. We then rebuild.

My story is about me, but I am not an island. My family, my friends, all factor in. In my case of this very tragic and public, personal event, how it was and is portrayed matters. The people and history involved matter. The situation and my response was complex. Therefore, my story may not fit into the mold of other memoirs and I wouldn't want it to.

Emily Dickinson, a standard bearer for poetry, was ridiculed for using capitals in her form a century ago. Time passes and we view things differently. What we write and share, changes norms, it reveals our evolution. Dickinson's style is now revered.

While I do not claim caliber worthy of Dickinson fame, I do understand what it means to break out of confines. I do know what it means to determine a life outside of your own and others' imaginings. To publish is an author's aim. Words in print, poured forth from an inner fount into readers' hearts and minds; that is the dream. My dream.

Several years were spent preparing and sending agent queries. Countless hours were spent researching the process, spent seeking representation or spent swallowing rejection (which became useful as a tool and a gauge). Energy poured into my edification of the "business". Publishing; that brass ring, the behemoth, is a maze to navigate and get lost in. My writing suffered before I realized that spending my finite time on attempting to get published narrowed a path that could not possibly funnel all authors to the top and did not guarantee a publishing contract. With good advice (and with countless Google searches) I have happily discovered my way to self-publishing. All that energy spent trying to fit in, cutting out, racing to be noticed, was zapping my creativity and starving my hunger for authenticity. Unwittingly, I was removing myself from my story- Until, midfall, I caught myself.

I questioned my goals and intentions. Then I questioned a system that was not designed for non-traditional writers, one that often depends on luck, a network or the tide of reader's tastes. That system, I decided, could not define my success. Courage and content could. So, I encouraged my inner work and coaxed words onto the page. In understanding how I was influenced, motivated, and best exploited, I began to think differently about how to avoid pitfalls, about ego and enhanced confidence. Best of all, I have returned to the place that brought my story forth, rejoicing in that original boost of potential, pride and possibility. There is no regret around my publishing journey. A heft of information taught me more about the industry (even it it was more than I wanted), and more about myself. With support I was affirmed in  stepping forward with self-publishing. Traditional publishing is an incredible accomplishment and I wish everyone on that path the best of luck. For my particular story, it became the heavy around my neck, a burden cursed by inexperience, by convention. I was the square hole in a world of round pegs.

Stepping fully into myself, with my own publishing imprint, my words, work and reward are my own. With an experienced editor's hand, my story, deemed unworthy of publication by some, will be told within my lifetime (unlike John Kennedy Toole, whose manuscript, *Confederacy of Dunces*, sat beneath his bed for eleven years before being found by his mother and published posthumously).

Writing a memoir is akin to writing your own eulogy or obituary (which I have done and though a bit dark, is a great writing and introspective exercise). To stand facing yourself squarely in a mirror, microscopically assessing every flaw, every achievement; a memoir attempts to find reason and expose the tragic optimism. Memoir asks why flaws are seen as imperfections, how conclusions are reached, how goals are achieved. Memoir demands a credit and account for yourself in each step and misstep.

> Your life has and will prepare you.

To sum up: **Tomorrows are in short supply.** We can worry about that, or we can accept our inevitability with peace and purpose. Worry reduces enjoyment, increases our stress and will not garner more time. No amount of worry will avoid our end. No amount of money will promise a sunrise. However, you do have this moment and can choose to live it to the fullest.

Personally, I hope to see you out there, living it up by your own standards. Find joy and seek purpose. Get to know yourself well, so that you can more deeply know others. And remember- **Kindness is a superpower.**

My life has prepared me to work, struggle, succeed, fail, succeed, fail, try, and try again. That is what survival comes down to. The effort. To wake each day and ask questions, seek knowledge and realize answers look different to each of us. That step forward sometimes means taking steps back. Blaming others for our scars, our defects, puts our responsibility solely on others; our parents, our ancestry, our leaders, environment, resources and upbringing. Find balance in responsibility. As we grow into ourselves, we are able to assess our own action or inaction, and to understand our privilege and place in life. There is no magic pill for staying above water when the floods come. It is my hope that however you swim through life, however you choose to stay afloat, that credit is given, to yourself and supporters, for each effort. Painful waves will wash over you. You have you made it this far. Keep swimming.

Hopefully we can extend sensitivity and grace to ourselves and others. Perhaps there is anger and forgiveness, action and peace.

**You will have to read my story someday to know...**

*With undying love for my family. And for Paris.*

# Personal Exercise

## PERSONAL EXERCISES BASED ON DYING TO KNOW MYSELF IN TIME

-Envision particular activities/people bringing joy.
-When has feeling rushed helped or hurt?
-When life hands you something hard,
  afford yourself time moving through responses.
-Is responding immediately necessary or helpful?
-Notice joy.
-Notice what brings about peaceful feelings.
-Observe others with curiosity.
-Discover famous quotes that resonate.
-Ask what has gone unsaid in your life.
-Walk/wheel/move in nature or in a city.
-Keep a journal by hand or use voice notes.
-Track your moods with the weather.
-Ask what is working in your life, and why.

## PICTURE YOUR LIFE IN FIVE YEARS.

## PICTURE YOUR LIFE RETIRED.

List 5 or more personality descriptors that speak to who you are:

Examples: Positive, Pensive, Antisocial, Confident, Quiet, Anxious, Talkative, Social Butterfly, Impatient. Methodical, Generally Concerned, Active, Activist, Rebel Loyal, Flighty, Resilient, Cautious, Sensitive, Emotional, Particular, Creative, Perfectionist, Fun-Loving, Balanced, Rooted, Overly Critical, Self Deprecating, Overly Confident, Introspective, Open...

List 5 qualities/characteristics you'd like to be remembered for:

Examples: Kind, Generous, Selfless, Successful, Wealthy, Ambitious, Had Nerve, Humorous, Empathic, Lone Wolf, Intelligent, Mediator, Ambassador, Strong, Athletic, Antisocial, Confident, Quiet, Centered, Methodical, Activist, Rebel, Loyal, Fun, Resilient, Thoughtful, Detailed, Attentive, Creative, Loyal, Fun-Loving, Prayerful, Spiritual, Reflective, Introspective, Open...

List 5 things you'd like to accomplish
before life is through:

Examples: Parasailing, Start a Business, Found a Non-profit, Hang Glide, Adopt a Child, Rescue all the Pets, Swim with Sharks, Own a House, Parent Children, Manage Fears, Better a Relationship with Family, Take Parent on Trip of a Lifetime, Run a Marathon, Buy a Farm, Travel to Mars, Own a Horse, Work a Vineyard, Work with People, Manage employees, Take Dance Lessons, Play on Survivor, Be a YouTube Sensation, Live in Wilderness, Spend a Month in Paris

## THE TELLING AND RECEIVING OF STORIES IN TIME:

Think of a story/book that stays with you.

Think about when you read it.

Who gave it to you or told it to you?

How did it impact you at that time or over time?

Is there a book you wish you had read earlier ?

Can you think of a story you may receive differently now?

What is a story you would easily share with someone less experienced in life?

What book, quote or poem have you repeatedly read or recommended?

What would the "story of your life" be about?

## WHAT WILL YOUR EULOGY SAY?